VENEZUELA

Keith Lye

Franklin Watts

London   New York   Sydney   Toronto

Facts about Venezuela

Area:
912,050 sq. km.
(352,145 sq. miles)

Population:
17,791,000

Capital:
Caracas

Largest cities:
Caracas (1,817,000)
Maracaibo (889,000)
Valencia (616,000)
Barquisimeto (497,000)
Maracay (440,000)

Official language:
Spanish

Religion:
Christianity

Main exports:
Oil and oil products,
iron ore, coffee, cocoa

Currency:
Bolívar

© Franklin Watts Limited 1988

Franklin Watts
12a Golden Square
London W1

Franklin Watts Inc.
387 Park Avenue South
New York, N.Y. 10016

ISBN: UK Edition 0 86313 645 1
ISBN: US Edition 0 531 10469 9
Library of Congress Catalog Card No:
87-51067

Maps: Simon Roulstone
Design: Edward Kinsey
Stamps: Harry Allen International
Philatelic Distributors
Photographs: Marion & Tony Morrison,
South American Pictures

Front & Back Cover: Tony Morrison

Typeset by Ace Filmsetting Ltd.,
Frome, Somerset
Printed in Hong Kong

The Republic of Venezuela, a country in northern South America, borders the Caribbean Sea. Many coastal villages contain houses built on stilts. These houses reminded early explorers of the Italian city of Venice, which is built on islands. They named the land "Little Venice", which in Spanish is Venezuela.

Two arms of the Andes Mountains run through northwestern Venezuela. They include the country's highest peak, the Pico Bolívar. This snow-capped mountain rises 5,002 m (16,411 ft) above sea level.

At the foot of the Andes Mountains is a low region called the Maracaibo basin. It contains Lake Maracaibo, the largest lake in South America. The Maracaibo basin is the country's most important oilfield.

The Guiana Highlands are in the southeast. Some of the mountains are flat-topped and are bordered by cliffs. These mountains inspired Sir Arthur Conan Doyle to write a book called *The Lost World*. In this book, he imagined that dinosaurs still lived on one of these mountains.

Venezuela's longest river, the Orinoco, has many tributaries which rise in the mountains. Waterfalls, such as the one shown here, are common in highland regions. The world's highest waterfall, Angel Falls, is in southeastern Venezuela. It is 979 m (3,212 ft) high.

Venezuela lies in the tropics and the lowlands are hot throughout the year. The mountains are cooler. The mountains and the south are rainy places. Thick forests cover large areas. But parts of the northern coast have little rainfall.

Between the dry coast and the hot
and wet southern forests is a region
called the llanos. This region has a
long dry season and much of it is
covered by tropical grassland with
scattered woodland. Cowboys graze
cattle on this grasland.

The picture shows some money and stamps used in Venezuela. The main unit of currency is the bolívar, which is divided into 100 céntimos.

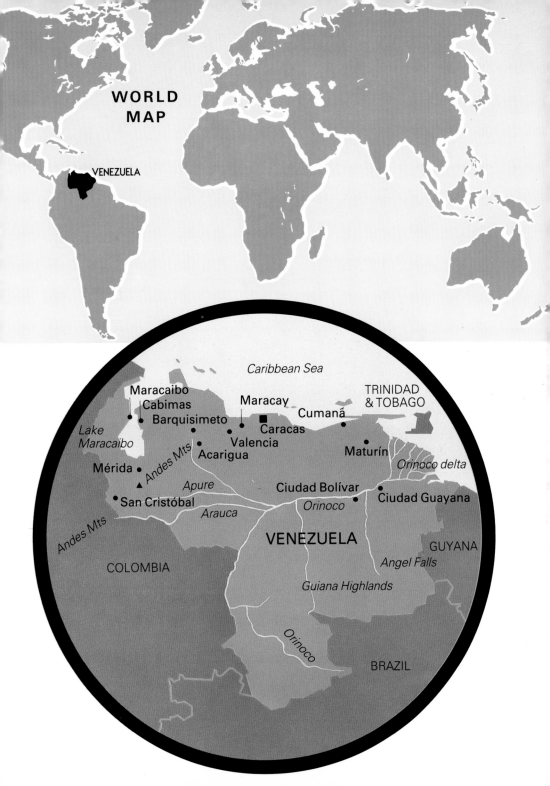

WORLD MAP

VENEZUELA

Caribbean Sea

TRINIDAD & TOBAGO

Maracaibo
Cabimas
Barquisimeto

Maracay

Cumaná

Lake Maracaibo

Caracas

Valencia

Maturín

Andes Mts

Acarigua

Orinoco delta

Mérida

Apure

Ciudad Bolívar

Ciudad Guayana

San Cristóbal

Orinoco

Arauca

VENEZUELA

Andes Mts

GUYANA

COLOMBIA

Angel Falls

Guiana Highlands

Orinoco

BRAZIL

The first people in Venezuela were American Indians. A few of them still live in remote areas, where they speak their own languages and follow ancient ways of life. But many have adopted western ways of life and speak Spanish.

The explorer Christopher
Columbus, sailing for Spain, landed
in Venezuela in 1498. He was
followed by others, including Spanish
settlers in the early 1500s. This statue
of Columbus is in Venezuela's
capital, Caracas.

The Spaniards brought black slaves to Venezuela. Over the years, the Indians, blacks and Spaniards have intermarried. Today, about two thirds of Venezuelans are of mixed descent. The others are of direct Indian, black or Spanish origin.

The Spaniards introduced
Christianity and built many churches,
such as this cathedral in Mérida.
Today, most Venezuelans are Roman
Catholics. There are about 20,000
Protestants. Spain ruled Venezuela
for about 300 years.

In 1811, the Venezuelans declared their country independent. But full independence was not won until 1821 when Simón Bolívar, a Caracas-born general, defeated the Spaniards at Carabobo, near Valencia. This is a painting of the battle.

16

Caracas was founded in 1567, but it is now a modern city. The gold-domed Capitol building is where the parliament meets. Venezuelans elect the President, who is Head of State and head of the government, and the Congress, which consists of a Senate and a Chamber of Deputies.

Maracaibo, Venezuela's second largest city after Caracas, contains the modern offices of the main oil companies together with old houses built in colonial times. About 85 per cent of Venezuelans live in cities and towns.

Barquisimeto, the fourth largest city (Valencia is third), has a modern cathedral. The cities contain many prosperous middle class people. But many Venezuelans are poor. Some live in unhealthy slums which have grown up around the cities.

Venezuela is rich in oil and oil makes up more than 90 per cent of the country's exports. Venezuela is the third most important oil producer in North and South America, after the United States and Mexico. This busy oil town is on the shore of Lake Maracaibo.

Other minerals include bauxite, coal, diamonds, gold, nickel and iron ore. The largest metal factories are in Ciudad Guayana, an industrial city founded in 1961. Cheap electricity is produced at hydroelectric plants in southern Venezuela.

Forests cover 21 per cent of the country and there are about 600 types of trees. Crops are grown on 4 per cent of the land, while grazing land makes up 18 per cent of the land area of Venezuela.

Farming employs 16 out of every 100 workers. Food crops include beans, maize (or corn), rice and wheat. Fresh produce is sold at markets in the towns. Coffee, cotton and sugar cane are major crops.

The most profitable type of farming is the raising of beef and dairy cattle. Venezuela has more than 12 million cattle which graze on large ranches in the llanos and in the Maracaibo basin.

Many people on the north coast earn their living by fishing. But Venezuela accounts for only 3 per cent of the total catch in South America. The picture shows men dividing up a small catch.

The government has recently improved its educational services. Education is now free and compulsory for nine years. Illiteracy is falling. In 1960, 37 per cent of Venezuelans could not read or write, as compared with 14 per cent in 1986.

The largest of the country's universities is the University of Caracas. The picture shows students playing basketball. Other popular sports are baseball and soccer. Some cities have bullfights and spectacular rodeos.

Standards of living among country people are steadily rising. The government is trying to improve services for country people, hoping that they will not move into the already overcrowded cities.

Cachapas, soft pancakes made
from corn meal (ground maize), are
a common food in Venezuela. Other
popular foods are bananas, black
beans, rice, poultry, fish and top
quality beef.

This picture shows Scouts
commemorating their national hero
Simón Bolívar in Ciudad Bolívar.
Young Venezuelans know that their
country's oil resources will run out in
20 years or so. But new wealth can be
created by hard work and the
founding of new industries.

Tourism is a growing industry. The coast has many beautiful beaches, such as Colorada Beach, near Cumaná. The country's metal reserves and its rivers, which can be used to produce hydroelectricity, are other natural resources which will be developed when the oil wells run dry.

Index